Clay it Forward

Turning Mud to Magic through Fire and Word

CASS CAMERON

Splash Tile Press
SAULT STE. MARIE, ONTARIO

Copyright © 2016 by Cass Cameron

All rights reserved. No part of this publication may be reproduced, distributed or transmitted in any form or by any means, without prior written permission.

Cass Cameron/Clay it Forward
174 Woodward Ave.
Sault Ste. Marie, ON P6A 3T7
clayitforward.ca

Publisher's Note: This is a compilation. Names, characters, places, and incidents are all used with permission. Locales and public names are sometimes used for atmospheric purposes. Any resemblance to actual people, living or dead, or to businesses, companies, events, institutions, or locales other than those who have given permission is completely coincidental.

Book Layout © 2016 BookDesignTemplates.com and Valerie King. You can contact Valerie for assistance at dramaking@shaw.ca

Clay it Froward/ Cass Cameron. -- 1st ed.
ISBN 978-0-9951654-0-3

For Bobby,
Forever my flame.

And for his legacy, with love:
Conor and Kim, Caitlin, Cydney and Cameron

May you honour all the story threads that brought you together in this tapestry of family and bear witness, with grace, to those that will unfold in your presence because of who you are.

Contents

Introduction 1
January - Golden Pride Rory's Beg, Borrow and Steal 11
February – Mental Health 19
March - Northern Fish Arts 27
April - Springtime 35
May – Mother's Day 52
June - Father's Day 64
July – Summertime 72
August - Danielle 76
September - Back to School 84
                The Ball Family 90
October - A Snurtle's Hallowe'en 96
November - Remembrance Day 102
December – Elventide 110

Introduction

Clay It Forward is the creation of an English teacher who for over 30 years has used her communication and literacy skills combined with the arts as a portal to engage learning. Clay it Forward was founded almost two years ago and is offered at over 25 events in Sault Ste. Marie, Ontario and area.

In the Beginning...

My first memories of "teaching" are with my sister. We were playing school, and she, although younger, was the leader: "You be the teacher, and I'll be the girl who does this." (*twirling her hair in ringlets*).

And so it was.

A shy and awkward thing, too tall, too skinny, bespectacled, soft-spoken, artsy and bookish, I was asked by teachers to stay in at recess to help students with missed spelling dictations.

I loved everything about the Nelson Spelling in Language Arts Series that was used when I was an elementary student in the late sixties and early seventies. They drilled the five aspects: phonics, spelling, vocabulary, grammar and writing. The hard-covered, modest books were a nice, humble size. The mostly white – ish top-half-cover was grimy with years' of kids' lead smudged finger prints all over. The bottom part of the book was always a different colour: a purplish blue – indigo? stands out in my mind: grade 7 perhaps (I remember being disappointed the entire year of the brown…grade 5?). Once cracked, the book opened to each new, but familiar lesson. Down the left of the page, in a faded version of whatever colour was on the front, was a one inch strip on which "the list words" appeared. Maybe 18 or 20 of them. Every 6 lessons was a "review" – and there were a whack.

Each regular lesson had the same predictable rhythm: Write each word three times each. Break them into syllables. Use them in a sentence. Then, do the activities in the lesson. Part A usually had some phonics rule that applied to a few of the list words: "i before e, except after c, or when sounding like a as in neighbour and weigh" … Part B, if I recall, was an extension of this activity. "Find three list words that end in "tle"…and so on….Most people found part E the torment: writing…."use at least 10 of the list words in a composition about….."

I was in heaven with all those words and rules and stories.

Later, in high school, the teachers would sit me beside the hooligans – hoping for a miracle of calming influence – and a passing grade.

The hooligans I got to know didn't much like spelling, or writing, or reading, or periodic tables…or much of anything to do with school – except the parts that repelled me: lunch and spare and the smoking area – or the gym and the football field.

But they had very interesting stories, living in worlds I knew little about. And since I wasn't a threat to the hooligan girls or a distraction to the hooligan boys, I got to know them all as just people with little of the drama that marks most high school navigations.

I went on to become a tutor for summer employment, took a degree in English literature and sociology, and accepted my first teaching position in Sault Ste. Marie in 1986, age 23.

My employer, Craig Reading & Educational Services, was a private enterprise offering academic upgrading to adults in transition. Our students were mostly WSIB clients, injured workers from the steel plant and paper mill, most of whom had gone to work directly out of high school and now needed refresher courses prior to returning to college and finding a new livelihood. They weren't too keen on school either.

They had great stories.

At the height of the program, before adult upgrading was taken over by the Ministry of Colleges, Training and Universities in the early 90's, I was one of three English teachers; one math teacher completed the staff to about 40 learners who attended – half of them in the morning, the other half in the afternoon.

The "school" was located above Morgan's Clothing, in Sault Ste. Marie, at the corner of Goulais Avenue and Second Line. My first apartment was right behind it. I could be at work in three minutes.

The students called it "Morgan High" and it was mostly a gas.

Our "curriculum" operated similarly to the Nelson Spellers from my youth. We had recipe cards for each student – each new card stapled to the one before, in alternating top corners as the days and weeks and months passed by, so, in time, the cards could be stretched out as great accordions of accomplishment while the students reprogrammed their brains and faced the music of their new, uncertain futures.

On the back of the first card, there again, were those "five aspects": spelling, phonics, vocabulary, language and grammar, and writing – comprehension rounded out the mix. Titles of the books, assigned to the learners' competency levels, were written under each heading.

Most of these students were guys – men with families and homes, usually "camps" too, and vehicles and comfortable, predictable lives. And they, as it turns out, were to be at the vanguard of a mass of workers sent back to school, not because they were injured and could no longer do their jobs, but because they were redundant and their jobs disappeared during the downsizing and corporate efficiencies of the 1990's.

Adult education, academic upgrading, retraining, second career, academic and career entrance – whatever ACE name one called that rose – became a cash cow for school boards and community colleges across the province and most of the country.

Our little program shut down.

I did some private tutoring, took up pottery, taught ESL and went to teacher's college, so I could be a "real" teacher and get a "real" job. But anyone who knows me will tell you I'm hardly based in reality and vice versa.

If Facebook had been around when I got my first job teaching "critical thinking" at the local community college, my "friends" would not just be "lol", they'd be "lmfao" hysterically. But I was domesticated now, with a mortgage, a spouse, two step-children, a baby girl, and a Malamute.

After over 15 years of contract work at the college, (now teaching the children of many of those first injured workers I'd met when I was fresh out of university), I was free in the most bizarre sort of way: the mortgage was paid, I was uncoupled, our youngest -another girl- was almost a teenager, and I was alive after emergency colon cancer surgery.

With no job security or work benefits at the college, I healed for a year on EI and took a job in absolute irony at an incoming call centre answering emergency requests for roadside assistance.

"lmfaolmfaolmfao!!!!"

I don't drive; I have no sense of direction and have no sense of urgency. But I can listen and type at the same time, I love hearing people's stories, I'm professional and empathetic and try "on my honour, to do my best, to do my duty, to God, the Queen and my country, to help other people at all times and to obey the Guide's law."

My mother was a Brown Owl and Guide Captain. I was a Gnome.

But this job – the only (barely-over) minimum-wage-job I'd had since high school – was also the only one I'd had of its kind in my life – permanent, full-time with benefits.

And it was humbling. I wasn't very good at first. I was terrible. I was slow and overwhelmed – I felt stressed and inadequate. I had to stay an extra week in the training class. I cried in the bathroom, humiliated; but at least I wasn't going to be fired. I knew for the first time what all those students for all those years had felt like. Totally out of my league.

The students were my co-workers now. Some were my supervisors. It was a bit awkward.

I knew their lives intimately; I'd read their essays for years; they were studying part-time. Some, astonishingly, were studying full-time. The company would pay local tuition for full-time students working full-time hours. Many had children. Others had graduated, but couldn't find work in their field, but had a mountain of student debt to repay, and cars to maintain, and dreams to try to keep flickering. Others were creatives: writers, musicians, actors, graphic novelists – clay artists. Feeding the muse with the day job.

But when the headset goes on and the lines open, it's all about the calls; if you can get your chops – which I finally, proudly did – it's a whole different kind of level playing field.

And the stories! From the customers needing jump starts, tows, tire-changes, winch outs, fuel deliveries, and the service providers we send out to help them; all the crazy predicaments we get ourselves into when we take that leap of faith and get into a car and drive...in a snowstorm...with no gas...and a Thanksgiving turkey...and children...in a strange city...with no insurance...and no money....there but for the grace....

When the cancer returned, I had to take a leave from work after almost three years.

I miss aspects of that job way more than I miss traditional teaching. It was so satisfying to know that after about three minutes, I could solve a person's problem, almost like magic; the system was in place and the car was towed – usually to the right place. On the other hand, I hated having to grade papers deeming one person an A+, another a C or an F. I hated being party to that humiliation and shame. I love words and language: I care about commas enormously, but I can live with myself much easier when I can show people how to do something to make their work better, rather than deducting half a point for a misplaced modifier and a full point for a run-on sentence and a sentence fragment.

At the call centre, as with the cancer, I entered an unfamiliar world that I had no bearings in.... but it's possible to get your chops in the strangest of places...with the most interesting of travelers along the way... and hearing the stories they will tell...

I've forgotten the name and the author of an essay we used to teach in ENG 110, but I remember the message: the point of an education, it argued, was not so much for the skills you would attain, or the employment doors that may – or may not – open (both of those are good points), but the main point was that, upon completion, you would know that you could finish something difficult. And having that faith in yourself would get you through a bunch of other tough things you'd be sure to encounter later on.

I remember one young woman at the call centre training class: while I was furtively taking pages and pages of notes like a court reporter, she was relaxed, funny, quick; she caught on to everything first; aced all the quizzes, but froze when we hit the floor to take live calls. Those first days were terrifying for us all, but she couldn't get over it. She couldn't let herself do it, and that will be one of the persistent stories she'll go through her life telling herself.

In my mind, as I heal again, I'm working on my opus: Colons, cancer and commas: healing through pause.

To that end, I submit my own clay curriculum with the same familiar aspects – the words, the phonics, the grammar and language – based always on the stories I encounter in my books, on my favourite radio shows or from the people I encounter.

I hope you find the delight and the comfort in your own way of learning for the rest of your life, listening to others' stories, and telling your own – and rewriting them and changing them up or changing the endings if they're no longer serving you. I hope you listen to your muse when she's dancing on your brain, and maybe trying your own hand at turning mud to magic through fire and word or joining us in safe, soft places to start hard conversations.

See you on the other side of the fire!

Cass

January - Golden Pride Rory's Beg, Borrow and Steal

Beg

We tried to teach him not to beg
We said.
But those eyes...

And the way he'd avoid your glance;
"I'm not really begging...
I'm just sitting here, keeping you company...
Looking over there...
...but if you happen to drop something?
I'll get it..."

Or the way he'd come in, after all those years
Still fresh and frisky from
Tearing along our side of the fence with Sam on the other side.
Old guys,
Volleying their testosterone taunts through the boards
'til someone called one of them off.

Then each, in his own yard,
Performed some victory ritual
Involving urine, a roll in the grass, a body shake
And a bound up the stairs.

I won.

Where's my treat?
It's not begging – I deserve it.

And away with a wag.

After dinner, on Saturday and summer mornings by his leash at the door –
Not begging, really...
Just waiting –
Always waiting.
For a pet, a look
Some time.

Borrow

Ghost walkers, the couple of years
Mostly just him and me now
Through all the old haunts in the neighbourhood
Where our pack used to roam –
Learning new to enjoy the solitary together;
To the pier, along the boardwalk, downtown, to the canal
Through porchy neighbourhoods, the schoolyard, the park
Just up and down the street if it's too cold or rainy or dark
Or he's limping.

Let him get the day's news from every tree and blade of grass.
More rituals.
Habit. Familiar. Comfort.

Even on that last walk
The perfect mid-summer's eve
A golden day's goodbye –
Warm, clear, beautiful;

He bounded like a puppy
Along the fence through the schoolyard
Off leash
Across Simpson
And down the cool, leafy alley...

He must have heard a silent call,
for he left us then, with a low, gentle howl
and joined his soul's pack
To find Gabby and Storm
And all the other's that we've loved,
Friends helped to wrap him
And bring him home
So we could take our leave.

Elizabeth made a card:
"dogs are only borrowed angels...

The pop-up inside was a bounding, winged golden
Bush-tail curved and glorious, ears a flight
Leaping after a fiery orb – a ball? the sun? a halo?

"...and it hurts when we have to give them back."

Steal

They steal the end of the couch
closest to the fire in winter
The sunniest spot on the deck in the summer,
Then the coolest shade;
Things best left in the garbage,
The woods,
The water

Kid's favourite toys
Too much of the bed

Our hearts.
The road before you seems impossible, chiseled from the rock. You work harder, pushing your body to tired exhaustion as you ascend to the top via virtual bicycle.

How to make dog bones:

1. Roll out clay to approximately 1/4 inch thickness.
2. Freehand, trace, or copy the bone of your choice.
3. Cut out bone, using pin tool
4. Study puppy treats for textures, stamps, ideas - or make up your own (Maybe write their name on it for a treasured keepsake)
5. Translate the markings to your dog bone using pods, bones, other found materials or rubber stamps to create design, texture and contour on your dog bone.
6. Smooth all edges. Use straw for placement of holes if used for hanging a wind chime, mobile, tree ornament or wall art.
7. Let dry, covered in plastic on newsprint until bone dry. (Pun absolutely intended.)
8. Bisque, glaze, high-fire.
9. Hang and enjoy. Consider creating a visual journal, hanging symbols of puppy's favorite treasures (balls, small stuffies, sticks, a piece of blanket, etc.) from the holes along the bottom of the bone.

Stencil concept for dog bones. Also consider using cookie cutters or any other bone shaped cutter.

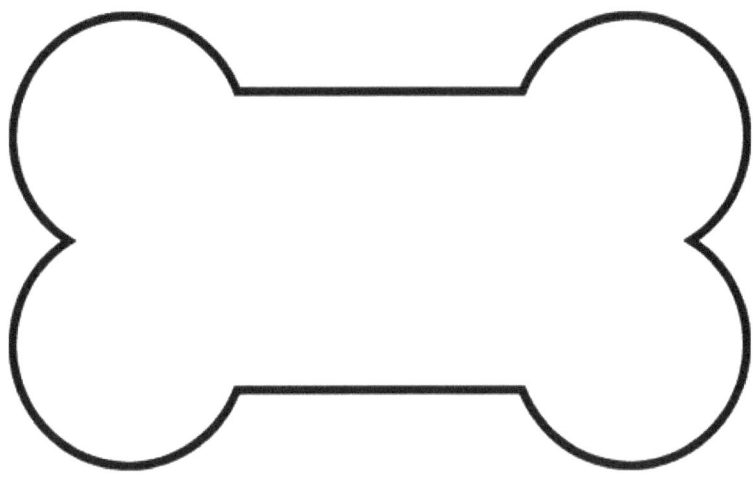

February

February – Mental Health

A friend wrote the following story about mental health and I liked it so much that I asked to include it.

Another story that spoke to me was the Black Dog of Depression. It can be found online at: https://www.youtube.com/watch?v=XiCrniLQGYc

The Worry Warts © by Valerie King

Once upon a time, in a place very similar to yours, with a life much like the one you live; there lived an ordinary person named Guy.

Guy was a pretty glad person. Things you might do for fun were fun to Guy. Everything Guy needed to live a glad life, he had; not too much and not too little.

One day, SOMETHING STARTLING happened. Guy wasn't expecting it at all.

It was a big surprise and it made his heart thump, and it made his muscles jump, and it made a funny burning lump grow in his chest. For a moment that felt like a long time, Guy didn't know what to do.

Should he freeze like an ice cube and hope the something passed him by without noticing him?

Should he flee like the fastest animal on earth and leave the something eating his dust?

Should he put on his big bad attitude and scare the SOMETHING away by screaming or fighting?

Guy wasn't sure...he hadn't encountered SOMETHING like this before.

That night, Guy told Protector about his encounter with the SOMETHING. Protector warmly patted Guy on the arm, gave him a big hug and said, "It's OK. You're just being a worry wart."

As Guy went to bed, he thought about being a worry wart and scratched his arm. There was nothing there, but he scratched anyway because being a worry wart sounded itchy.

The next day, Guy was out walking and saw SOMETHING ELSE. He remembered the SOMETHING from yesterday.

His heart went thump, and his muscles went jump, and this time he got a burning in his throat as he held back tears.

Guy scratched his arm and turned down a new street to avoid SOMETHING ELSE. Almost right away, another spot on his arm started itching.

There was nothing there, but it itched anyway.

"I think I might have the Worry Warts," Guy said.

Every day Guy ran into SOMETHING NEW. Every day, SOMETHING OLD seemed to change into SOMETHING SCARY.

Guy started to avoid walking down his favorite street. He started avoiding going to his favorite places to eat. He even started itching on the bottoms of his feet!

Guy started to look ill. He worried that the water was giving him Worry Warts, so he stopped bathing. He worried that cotton was giving him Worry Warts, so he only wore his gym shorts and a nylon jacket.

Soon, Protector noticed that Guy was unwell and suggested he visit the Doctor.

Guy was scared. What if the Doctor told him that he had Worry Warts? By this time, Guy was itchy all the time.

His heart thumped all the time. His muscles bumped ALL the time. And he always had a tummy ache or a throat ache...or both!

Protector held Guy's hand while they waited for the Doctor.

Doctor was really nice. Doctor listened to Guy's story and smiled understandingly.

Guy wasn't a worry wart. Guy didn't HAVE Worry Warts. Guy had a condition called Generalized Anxiety Disorder... GAD. Doctor explained it was like GLAD without the L. So Guy wasn't feeling glad, because he had started living life without his L.

Doctor had two solutions for Guy. First, they told Guy that medication could help him be brave enough to find his L. Second, Guy was given an appointment to talk to a Counsellor to help him learn to find, and then keep, his L.

Guy was nervous. What if the medication made the itching worse? What if the Counsellor said he was REALLY sick and needed to be in the hospital? Protector helped Guy feel brave by giving him lots of hugs. Protector listened to Guy's fears with great big listening ears, a warm smile, and not a lot of words; because feelings need a LOT of listening.

After sharing his fears with Protector, Guy took the medicine. When the day came, Guy saw the Counsellor. The Counsellor helped Guy learn how to keep a tool box of skills close for the times when he needed to fix his GLAD. Sometimes the L would fall out of that word for confusing reasons, but with his tools, Guy could fix his GLAD. Some of the tools included breathing slow, deep breaths; going for walks with Protector; and getting enough sleep at night. Counsellor told Guy the tools could be a bit different for everyone.

And you know what happened? Over time, Guy noticed that when SOMETHING STARTLING happened, Guy reacted with just the right amount of worry; not too much and not too little.

And Guy walked down his favorite street again. He went to his favorite place to eat again.

And best of all, Guy stopped being itchy on his feet again! Guy had learned that not everything would cause him harm...and the Worry Warts were gone.

Disclaimer

The Worry Warts don't happen the same for everyone. Generalized Anxiety Disorder has many ways of presenting, based in many ways of being human. Symptoms and treatments also vary from person to person. Some people need medication, others do not. Some people need intense therapies, others do not. Please do not self-diagnose, or self-medicate. Always work with the professional of your choice to get the best combination of support for you. Many communities have free consultation services through organizations like Canadian Mental Health Association and Algoma Family Services.

How to make your own dog in modelling clay

1. Make the Parts: You need a Body (this will look like a sausage), 4 feet (they look sort of like candy corn), a tail (a small sausage proportional to the body), a muzzle (a can-shaped piece smaller than the body), a nose (a small pea), 2 eyes (think whites with dots on them), a tongue (flat and small), and 2 ears (I like floppy ones)
2. Assemble the Parts: The muzzle goes on the front of the body near the bottom. The eyes go above the muzzle. The ears on either side. The feet below. The tail behind. You know what a dog looks like.
3. Add markings and a collar
4. Finish off with fur marks, eyebrows, and whisker dots
5. Make your dog look as unique as you want – it's YOUR dog.
6. Enjoy

March - Northern Fish Arts

Pisces: February 20- March 20.
When my sister and I were much younger, perhaps (she) 8 and (me) 10, we received gifts from - I'm not sure whom - Grandma and Papa? that first introduced us to our astrological signs.

They were narrow, house-shaped, Papier Mache money boxes with a slit on the top to put the coins in, and a rubber-stoppered hole on the bottom to get them out.

No doubt there were a couple of coins put in with some stern, Scottish admonition to "save them for a rainy day."

They must have been souvenirs from a trip, that we'd get them both at the same time: hers was a bright, spring green, with two bluish, purplish fish - Pisces for her March 8 birthday. Mine was yellow with a pair of boy and girl twins - Gemini for my cusp-ish, June 20 naissance.

I liked hers better.

Around the same time - we were living on the twelfth concession in Severn Bridge, just outside of Orillia - I remember a traumatizing ice-fishing expedition that put me off the sport forever.

My dad and his friends were great ice-fishing fans. They'd put their huts out on Lake Couchiching and spend winters in festive, sweaty camaraderie - rules of all sorts being considerably more lax than today's.

On sunny, winter weekends, the families would get dragged along on these outings, down to the lake - kids and dogs and a day's provisions packed into the yellow ski-boose pulled behind the yellow ski-doo. We'd join the caravan of neighbours headed out to the middle of the lake.

I didn't like anything about these outings.

The sun's glare on the snow killed my eyes, then I was further blinded by the gloom inside the dark hut. I couldn't see anything. My glasses were always in some state of fogginess between the hot-breath condensation through the picky scarf outside in the cold, to the steamy film that crept up the lenses when the heat from the stove hit them once we'd all piled inside.

Getting there, I found the very notion of snowmobiling over a lake - especially the slushy edges - very distressing; inside the hut, that gaping hole down to frigid green eternity even more so.

For a person whose favourite place is off to the side, quietly observing, I found the boisterous, crowded togetherness of these events taxing. Inside the hut, we'd be squeezed onto the bench, two adults and a kid or vice-versa, trying to get warm - the science of the situation soon worked its magic: hot stove, pink insulation, one-piece snowsuits and a closed door soon had everyone peeling of layers and trying to get out.

And so the day was a jostling of in and out, always at the mercy of the extremes: sweating or frozen, blinding light or gloom. The mothers would have arranged games and activities...food. Outside in the glare and cold, we'd take turns pretending to drive the quiet, hulking machines, or make a fort in the ski-boose.

We would have to try our hand at fishing down a hole someone had bored through the ice and scoop out the icy chunks with a great, galvanized slotted ladle. I was terrified to fall into one of these, too.

When the day mercifully ended, we could finally get home to civility: a fireplace, food cooked in a kitchen, served on a plate. Then a dry, warm bed - alone, finally, with a book.

One trip was especially memorable before that final reward.

Someone, my dad, probably, had caught a huge fish - a pike? Pickerel? Something with a P, I think. Everyone was greatly excited, but to get the great, hulking thing home, they laid it along the running board of the snow machine and somehow I had the honour of riding behind my dad.

I had to watch my foot, that I didn't squish....dinner?

When we finally got home, they put it in the bathtub and everyone came over to have a look, take pictures. Tub time has never been the same.

This episode was only overshadowed by a smelting event, where, in my nocturnal blindness and abysmal sense of balance and direction, I ended up in the drink.

After enduring a wet, cold, endless ride home, I still had to watch the next day - and help, no doubt - as the great pail of silvery wiggles (these were the days when the smelts REALLY ran in great, midnight torrents...) was dumped on a thick wad of newsprint for "cleaning" - a misnomer for the gruesome evisceration and separation of head and tail from body.

Then pan fried dinner.

Nasty business. All.

My Piscean pleasures lie, instead, with tropical aquaria - or better yet, books and documentaries of underwater worlds of colour, beauty, grace and life.

I can appreciate the appeal of sport fishing; I've certainly heard many an enthusiastic tale and read my share of fish fables and stories in literature, but the muscular, violent, predatory struggle ending in death on a plate is too grim for me on the whole, so I amuse myself, instead, with making funky fish likenesses in clay.

Here's how: graceful, colourful and alive
Sport fishing, muscular, violent, predatory, struggle and death lifeless, least favourite of the short story themes: man vs. Nature

Clay fish tiles in 10 steps

Made for Arts at Bay, Arts at the Dock, Uli's Bay, Fishbowl Festival, various summer arts and culture events.

1. Roll out clay to approximately 1/4 inch thickness.
2. Freehand, trace, or copy the fish of your choice.
3. Cut out fish, using pin tool
4. Study the anatomy, markings, fins and proportions of real species - or make up your own (I like to start with Dr. Seuss!)
5. Translate the markings to your fish using mesh bags for scales, shells, pods, bones, other found materials or rubber stamps to create design, texture and contour on your fish.
6. Smooth all edges. Use straw for placement of holes if used for hanging a wind chime, mobile or wall art.
7. Let dry, covered in plastic on newsprint until bone dry.
8. Bisque, glaze, high-fire.
9. Hang and enjoy. Consider creating a visual journal, hanging summer treasures (stones, shells, feathers, sea glass etc.) from the holes along the bottom of the fish.
10. Consider some alternatives: Instead of cutting out the fish, create a platter, dish or bowl by impressing a fish design on the slab of clay and slumping it over a dish or stone for contour. Use fish tile as a bun warmer, hot plate, wall art or serving tray. Affix to splash tile in kitchen or bath. Enjoy!

April

April - Springtime

Everyone is twitterpated in springtime as someone points out in Bambi.

With three girls in the house, we spent many years watching almost every Disney movie created. My stepdaughter (who, even now at age 30, is probably going to fork over big money to get a copy of Cinderella out of the Disney vault) was the ring-leader, and my mother, a co-conspirator, brought every new release with the annual Easter visit, and the winter princesses awaited us on Christmas visits to Orillia.

When I first found out our twitterpation was bringing us a spring baby, I wrote this piece for my stepson, Conor, who had quiet, mixed emotions about sharing his dad with a new step-sibling.

The original manuscript had Conor's name, but I changed it to Moose in a revision some years ago when I created the Moosicians and considered using those clay characters as illustrations to the story one day:

"We're going to have a what?!!" He said,
"A baby Moose; now hop in bed,
We'll talk about it for awhile
His dad said, with a gentle smile.

But Moose, quite stunned, took three steps back
And looked upon the this maniac.

"Talk! What talk?"

What can you mean?
I'm feeling sick!
I'm turning green!
I'm shocked! I'm crazed!
I'm quite amazed!
I'm feeling faint
I'm feeling dazed!

I'm flabbergasted! Overcome!
In fact, my body's all gone numb!
This news, I've not anticipated!
Oh, Dad!
I'm discombobulated!"

And Moose, now drained,
Sunk to the floor,
A crumpled mess,
Could say no more.

The father moved beside his son
And took him in his arms
He'd done
the best he could to break the news;
He'd minded all his p's and q's

Young Moose, he pulled tight
To his chest,
Exhausted both,
They fell to rest.

Sleep came quickly to Moose Boy

And with it that familiar joy
Of peace and warm tranquility...
Beside his dad - security.

But then, well-known and pleasant dreams
Of hockey pucks and all-star teams
Were interrupted, stopped, reword,
Abruptly ended; grounded down.

Into his very own dream's eye
Came uninvited, like a spy
A creeping, crawling, creature wild,
A drooling, small, moose-monster child!

It looked him up and down, and then
It plunked itself on its tail end.
It cooed and babbled, smiled and burped,
It clapped its hooves, and squealed and slurped

And then! - of all the nerve! The gall!
It reached for his new tennis ball! It seized it with its tiny paw
And shoved it in its toothless maw!

It gnawed upon the yellow fuzz,
Contented, happy - just because!
But Moose-Boy, quick as any cat
Retrieved the thing,
But after THAT,
He looked as though he ate a lime...
His ball dripped wet with BABY SLIME!

While Moose-Boy wiped his hooves quite dry,
The Monster-Child, more things did spy;
It headed for the trophy shelf
And surely planned to help itself!

But since that shelf was out of reach,
It settled for the things beneath;

The building blocks
And baseball cards
The hockey pucks and
Skate-blade guards,
The treasured books, the stuffed giraffe,
The famous players' autographs

It was too much for this poor fellow!
He'd had enough; he had to bellow:

"Get out! Get Out! Get Out! I say!
You must leave now! You cannot stay!
You've made a mess in this short time!
You've slimed on EVERYTHING that's MINE!"

The young Moose-Child then turned its head;
it sucked its lip and turned quite red.
It shook and trembled like a leaf
While Moose-Boy stared in disbelief.

Before his very eyes, it changed,
Transforming, like it had the mange!

It's small, bald head and blotchy face
A certified disgrace!

Then from that large and gaping hole
Came forth a horrid sound.
A howl so loud and powerful
That Moose-Boy looked around,

To see if it could really be
This baby that eruptcd...
It was! Oh wow! What noise! And how
His ears had been corrupted.

Then tears so big and full and round
Came tumbling down its cheeks,
Dripping, splashing to the floor;
You'd think it sprang two leaks!

And Moose-Boy stood and stared in awe
Transfixed - he could not move -
He needed to go get his Pa -
His point - at last! - to prove.

Just then, he heard his father's step
Come briskly up the stairs.
"Oh, good!" he thought,
"Now here's relief!
You'd better say your prayers.

You've had it now! Your goose is cooked!
You've had your last hurrah!

You're done! You're THROUGH! You're outta here!
You've plucked my dad's last straw!

He was about to tell his dad this trauma he'd been through,
When, to his room, came hurrying, a guy he hardly knew.

This Moose! His Dad! Brushed right past HIM!
Right to that sobbing thing!
He picked it up and held it close
And then...BEGAN TO SING!

A lullaby, a gentle song -
Oh! This was all SO WRONG!
The world's gone MAD! It's BAD! It's SAD!
Now where did HE belong...?

Just then, Moose-Boy was wakened
By his radio alarm
His brain was fogged, his hoof asleep;
He'd slept on his left arm.

He had to shake his boggled head;
What was that he'd been dreaming?
What dream! That was a NIGHTMARE, kid!
With that incessant screaming!

Down from his bunk, he dressed, made bed,
Performed his toiletries,
Then sat outside, confronting

All his insecurities.

His dad found him just sitting there, lost in a reverie
"Can I sit down?"
"Sure, Dad," he frowned.
"You still have time for me?"

"Of course, I do! It's me!....It's you!
That's never going to change
"Oh, yeah?" asked Boy.
"Then why've you gone and done this thing so strange?

You're tired of me! What have I done?
You've dumped me, I'm afraid.
You're starting new! That's it; we're through!
Oh, Dad! I've been betrayed!"

Moose-Dad looked Boy right in the eye
And gave him one hard stare.
"Now just you wait a sec, young Moose;
We have to clear the air.

You'll always be my first-born son,
your sister, my first girl.
This next...whatever it might be...
The mystery will unfurl.

You know I'm not a sappy guy;
I'm not that big on mush,
But what I have to say right now
Bears list'ning to; so hush:

This large moose heart of mine, like yours,
Is big enough, you see
To love a dozen moose - or more -
No problem, then, with three!

This love-stuff is a wild, weird thing
Its power can astound -
It's not as though we only have
So much to go around.

Now even though this baby's
A surprise to all concerned,
There's one thing that I know for sure,
From you two kids, I've learned

That each one brings a bunch of love
Before it breathes in air
To spread upon the lives with which
It finds it's going to share.

I know you think that this new one
My love from you will steal.
You think I'll love you less - for him -
That's natural to feel.

But life just doesn't work that way
He'll need me tons, that's true;
He'll zap my time and energy...
Believe me! You did, too!

But you and me? We're stuck, for life,
Connected through and through -
Not one darned thing - moose, word or deed
Can change my love for you.

This baby will belong to US
As much to you as me.
It need you - it needs ALL of us
To grow up right, you see?

Another thing you need to know,
Now that this gush is doe,
Don't think for just one second
That it's going to be all fun....

Those mushy folk will ooooh! And aaaaahh!
Get weepy, soft and smarmy,
Speak of sentiment and miracles...
The sap could stop an army!

Those babies are a ton of work;
Life's over as we know it.
They smell, they drool, they cry, they sleep.
And thanks? They never show it.

They're sweet; at times, hilarious,
And cute and all that stuff;
But most of all, they get their kicks
By making our lives rough!

These babies do not have respect -

they rule the roost - cause riot.
They disregard all notions of
Your need for peace and quiet.

Their egos are enormous,
Scoffing at your rights and freedoms.
You can trust me with these baby facts:
Years back....you used to be one!

But you grew up, turned out all right.
I loved you then - still do.
T'was the same way with your sister,
I'll survive this next one, too.

I'll love you all, none more, none less,
Each in a special way.
Someday, this might make much more sense;
That's all that I can say."

"Thanks, Dad," Moose-Boy said to his Pop
"I'll think about these words.
I hope they soon make sense'
Right now, I think it's for the birds!"

He peeked into the laundry room;
She stood there folding clothes.
How was it she had grown this big
Before his very nose?

Her belly jutted out so far!
How had he been so blind?

She never used to look like this
From front or from behind!

She looked at him; she knew he knew
And asked, "Are you alright?"
"I'm not quite sure," he said to her;
"I had strange dreams last night."

"I have them, too."
"You do?"
"It's true," she reassured him then
"I'm still in shock myself," she said.
"You are?"
"You bet I am!

I'm happy, sad and terrified,
Confused and dazed - excited.
I'm scared, depressed and horrified,
Rejoicing and delighted.
I'm moody, mad, hysterical,
I'm feeling out of whack
I'm feeling blue; yet tickled pink
And not to mention, FAT!"

The next few days passed by alright
He got on with his life
With moments here and moments there
Of happiness and strife

Then finally, that big day arrived;
They switched to panic mode.

And just in time! Moose-Mama
Looked as though she might explode!

"It went well at the hospital."
Dad told him on the phone.
"They're both OK; I love you, Son.
And soon they brought it home...

He looked upon the tiny thing
Who looked right back at him.
It waved a hoof; then, closed its eyes
And cracked a gassy grin.

And right before his own mind's eye,
Some visions flashed on by...
He saw himself in future days
Alongside this small fry:

The holidays he'd share with him;
The way he'd teach him how
To throw a curveball, stop a puck,
Read books, ride bikes, and now....

He saw himself teach this young tyke
The things he'd have to know:
Pitch tents, catch fish, build forts, make sleds,
Mush Malamutes through snow.

Somehow it didn't matter that
They had a different mother;
This helpless thing, new to the world,

Was his own little brother.

His dad still was his dad, he knew
His sister - the same, too.
His brother's mom was her same self -
Much slimmer now, 'twas true

And he? Well, he felt much the same,
Yet different, too, somehow;
Older, bigger, more mature,
Important, wise....and proud.

"Well," he mused, (there seemed to be
The need for some word said.)
"I guess he's here to stay for good,"
He stroked the soft, bald head.

"But let's get two things straight, on which
I'll never change my tune:
I won't change dirty diapers,
And HE CAN'T COME IN MY ROOM!"

In our family, the moose child turned out to be a girl, my first daughter, Cydney, followed almost four years later by her baby sister, Cameron.

Conor is a great, big brother to all three of his sisters.

How to make a Moose in Modelling Clay:

1. Make the Parts: Head like a peanut with a dent in the end, body like a big almond, tail like a small spaghetti, a flat pancake for the base, 4 cone legs, a small pancake for the lip, 2 ears, 2 eyes with eyebrows above them, and 2 antlers.
2. Assemble the pieces: Put the base down, place the 4 legs on the base with reference to the body, place the body on the legs, place the head on the body
3. Add the tail on the back, place the eyes on the top of the head closest to the body, and place the lip under the nose dent.
4. Finish by adding the antlers and giving the moose some ears.
5. Now you can put on a little fur, put hooves on the ends of the feet by gouging out a little line, and VOILA! You have a moose

May – Mother's Day

The first Fusion Clay and Glass conference I went to several years ago resulted in a new direction for handmade mugs for me.

As part of the conference, a "mug-exchange" table was set up, and each potter could "trade" one mug for another. All mugs were "hidden" in stapled paper bags, so selections were a surprise.

In the potters' world, a bit of a divide - or at least a distinction - exists between wheel throwers and hand-builders: throwers use the potters' wheel to centre a lump of clay and pull it into form. Think "Ghost", 1990, with Patrick Swayze, Demi Moore and Whoopi Goldberg. It's rhythmic, centred, precise, fluid, functional.

Hand-building - using slab, pinch, coil and combinations - to my way of thinking, is more abstract, intuitive, impulsive, sculptural and sensual in different ways. Think Gaudi.

I am a hand-builder.

Both wheel throwing and hand building have architectural elements: master potter, Robin Hopper, observed at the 2006 Fusion Conference in North Bay that architects are makers of pots for people....

Tea pots and the attendant mugs are staples in the potters' repertoire for both throwers and builders.

The mug I traded was a nice enough thing. Slab, with turtle stamps I had hand-carved in coin-sized rounds of plaster. It was aesthetically pleasing, glazed in a commercial greenish-blue, called "Copernican Sky" if memory serves.

The mug I received was slab, too. But the glaze treatment sent my work in a new trajectory. The slab had been rolled with a mesh, and impressed with an assortment of found objects. After bisque firing, the mug was dipped in a cobalt glaze and the blue was wiped off the mesh pattern to reveal the white clay below, leaving the blue deep in the crevices created by the mesh and other impressions.

This contrast, not only in colour, but also in texture and surface treatment appealed to me immensely, and I studied it further in a workshop with Chandler Swain at a subsequent Fusion Conference in Toronto.

And so were born my "Rainbow Wash" mugs, a staple in my Clay in the Classroom program and Mugs Shots career and community profiles series.

With an assortment of texture-makers, including mesh and lace, an ever-expanding tool basket of rubber stamps and found objects including bones, shells, twigs and anything else that makes a cool impression in clay, we make designs in the clay.

After bisque, I brush on a rainbow of under glazes, then wipe them off, so the colours blend into each other and stay in the cracks and crevices of the design, against the bright white of the stoneware or porcelain. Then I apply a coat of transparent for the final high fire and am de-lighted every time with the results.

So are the students - and their mothers who receive them as Mother's Day gifts.

The Mother's Day mug projects have become a bitter-sweet occasion over the past few years.

The last time my parents visited me together, it was Easter of 2011 and I was doing an Earth day event that my mom was helping with. I was just getting back to workshops after a year or so off after cancer surgery, treatment and recovery.

My mom had never witnessed me "in my element" with clay since I've lived - for half my life - eight hours away "from home".

It took me by surprise - and it's a treasure I hold dear to this day - when I overheard her whisper to a parent, "That's my daughter, the artist."

My parents, like most, were most relieved when I was gainfully employed on a teaching contract either with the board or the local community college, "getting my foot in the door", but my entire "career" was always a bit tenuous, to their way of thinking.

This art thing...certainly I had talent, but...is it really worth it, honey?

Maybe I should put it on the back burner while I worked more on getting a real job?

While we never spoke of it, I'm certain she had concerns that not only did I inherit my birth father's genetically flawed connective tissue disorder - Marfan's Syndrome - that could potentially see me drop dead any second of a ruptured aorta as he did at age 27 leaving her a widow at 25 with two young daughters - but,

He wasn't keen on real jobs either, it seems.

"He was a good father; he loved you girls very much.""

That was the standard answer we got whenever my sister and I asked about this mystery man.

Over the years, I've sleuthed out about ten facts that I hold to tightly, as Opal does in Kate Di Camillo's "Because of Winn-Dixie" when she makes her father tell ten

things about her mother, who left them when the girl was very young.
He had laughing eyes
He had great dimples
He had thick, wavy, dark hair, like mine
He was a glass blower
He moved a lot
He couldn't hold down a job
He knew a lot of waitresses' names
He was a Pisces
He drove around at night looking for burnt out neon signs to fix.
Deduction: he was an artist and entrepreneur
As mother's will, mine walked, I'm certain, that line between several truths in order for her daughters to keep an image - and what sliver of a memory they may have held - of their lost Daddy, a hero.
I've heard it said that a woman reaches a new maturity when her own mother dies.
If so, my sisters and I "grew up' the summer of 2012, and, desperate to harness all the wisdom and suffocating love we so recklessly took for granted all our lives, we still find ourselves impossible matriarchs of our own little dynasties.
I have a new level of appreciation now, as a mother without a living mother, when I make Mother's Day mugs.
Putting pen to paper after she crossed the curtain, I thought first and only about the loss of her leaving, but I couldn't abide that loneliness and finality.
And it wasn't true;

Even though we had lost her physically, we could find her in so many more ways, if we were open to looking, and seeing and feeling and being.
I choose finding over losing, any day.
(My niece, Kristin, couldn't say "grandma", so my mom was forever "mama" to all her grandchildren)

Finding Mama

In memory of Dianne Dorothy (Edgar) (Cameron) Hodge
December 11, 1940 - July 12, 2012
Who taught us how to pray:

God Bless

Mommy and Daddy

And

Jackie & Sandy & Judy & Michelle

Grandmas & Papas & Nannies

Aunties & Uncles and Cousins,

Girlfriends & Boyfriends

Make me a good girl,

Amen

Often,

I'd turn around,

And

She'd be gone

Just dis-ta-peared!

But then,

I'd look again,

And I'd find her

...in the store, taking back shoes;

...racing toward us to get in the picture;

...in the bush, collecting rocks;

...on the sidelines, cheering on kids;

...at the back of the bus, thwacking some bully

...in the wings, sending people on stage;

...in her garden, controlling weeds;

...in the water, diving for lost glasses

Or

Teaching some kid how to canoe, water ski or swim

"Bloop!"

Then that day,

She dis-ta-peared again.

For good.

Gone

Couldn't find her anywhere.

And everyone reached out,

through the LEXICON OF LOVE

Anguish, Bereavement, Condolences, Departed, Eternity, Faith, Grace, Hope, Infinity, Joy, Kindness, Loss, Memories, Now, Owls, Prayer, Quietude, Respect, Sympathy, Trust, Us, Vulnerable, Wonderful, xxoxoxo, yearning, zzzzzen.

Then I heard myself say something familiar;

Recognized her face in my mirror;

Her presence in my sisters and my aunties,

Her spirit in our children;

Heard her voice - and tone - in ours;

Played the spoons;

Felt the breeze through the leaves

Listened to kids' laughing;

Believed in healing;

Remembered a song;

Forgave an old grievance;

Told a familiar story;

Took a picture;

Rode a streetcar;

Started a project - then finished it;

Made a list;

Believed in myself;

Loved my children - and all their friends;

Sat by the river;

Held a stone;

Saw faces and shapes in clouds and rocks and trees;

Enjoyed solitude - and company.

Made a phone call;

Wrote a letter

Connected with friends;

Had a good cry;

Then we

LAUGHED!

For

Even though

She's

NOWHERE,

I FIND HER EVERYWHERE

How to make a clay mug:

1. Roll out clay to 1/2 in thick.
2. Cut a rectangle that will fit around your "mug" form (soup can, cardboard tube, jar, etc.)
3. Cut a circle to fit slightly beyond the diameter of the "mug" and a "c" shape for the handle.
4. Use stamps, texture and found items to decorate your mug
5. Put your initials and date on the bottom of the base.
6. Wrap newsprint around the "mug" form; wrap clay rectangle over newsprint
7. Seal edge with a bit of water. Attach "C" handle and circle base
8. Ensure all edges are smooth and sealed.
9. Remove form. Smooth a thin coil of clay on inside base edge of mug

Dry. Bisque. Glaze. High fire. Enjoy.

Thanks, Mom! Cheers

June - Father's Day

Father's Day is another popular day for Clay in the Classroom.

We've made many mugs, trophies, sports sculptures and assorted other projects to acknowledge the bond between father and child.

There's always a bit of trickiness and sensitivity around Mother's Day and Father's Day for the children whose parent is absent from their lives, or who has recently passed or with whom they have a poor relationship. We dance around that by saying, "...or another person that' special to you such as a grandparent, relative, sibling or friend."

I'm especially sensitive to the Father's Day project. My own birth father died when I was three and my sister was an infant, of a ruptured aorta - or "aortic dissection" as a result of Marfan's Syndrome, a congenital condition of a connective tissue disorder that I inherited from him as well.

I've learned that "it's a thing" for children of deceased parents to fret, consciously and unconsciously, about dying of the same thing - especially when the child reaches the same age as the parent when they died.

That was certainly true for me.

Throughout my life I harboured intense, quiet, morbid fears of all kinds of unbecoming ends. It was a wordless hypochondria whenever I heard of any diseases or outbreaks (I remember the terror I felt during the summer of the "killer bees" scare when I was ten or so), and I remember feeling intense panic and anxiety whenever my mother had a doctor's appointment, so frightened was I that she would be diagnosed with some horrible affliction and die too.

I was married when I was 27, the age my father died, and my husband knew my fears of not being long for this world.

When our two daughters came along, little sisters for my step-son and step-daughter, my anxiety quietly persisted, especially when all four were in my care at the same time. I worried not only for the "regular" fears of crib death, childhood diseases and unthinkable home accidents - that I would undoubtedly have caused - but also for that genetic crap shoot of the Marfan's

Somehow we all survived.

Now that I am past the half century mark, with my aorta still intact, I feel a freedom and peace I could never have known as a child. I know that death is the end cover to each book of life. I have borne what was once the unthinkable: the loss of treasured pets, the deaths of close family members, a best friend, my mother, my second father, and very recently, my un-husband.

I have been at death's door on a few occasions, including cancer, but it has not yet opened for me, and I am grateful for every day on this side of the curtain.

Watching his four children mourn their father's loss at ages 35, 30, 21 and 18, I am overcome by their dignity, class and love for a man with whom everyone had a complex relationship.

This past Christmas, our two youngest daughters received this card from their dad, along with a gift of a *travel book and money for each of their ten-year passports:*

Hello, Merry Christmas, Selon le vent!

As the wind takes me; Samuel Beckett, an Irish writer I admire, wrote those words.

The wind did not take him too far. He contented himself with living and writing in France, mostly Paris. I planned to call my sailboat that would take me around the world - Selon le Vent, but that has not happened - not yet!

I have always had wanderlust. I love to travel and experience new cultures and different places. Some of that may have been inherited from my grandfather, your great grandfather, who left England as a young man to see the world by ship. He eventually arrived in Canada and made it his home, and I am grateful.

Conor and Caiti have that trait too. Caiti went to South Africa for a year, and you know about Conor's many canoeing and kayaking adventures in the Canadian wilder-ness.

I used to worry about them when they went off on voyages of discovery, but not so much anymore because I think they know how to take care of themselves and to keep safe.

Fathers have a paternal instinct to protect their children, and I am no different. The farther away my children, the less I feel able to protect them.

I suppose you two will want to have your adventures also. That is a good thing, and I want you to have those experiences. I just want you to be safe. I hope this book, (The Big Trip.......), which is full of information for travelers, will help you plan your trips, and reassure your parents that you are not taking any risks! And you will always have your home in beautiful Canada to return to. I think that is something you will learn from travel too.

I love you both beyond words and am immensely proud of you.

Love,
Dad

In a culture of "inking" that I don't understand, I was, again, overcome when the girls decided to have their dad's sailboat and words tattooed under their hearts, forever linking them with each other and with him as they travel their lives' journeys.

Cydney drew his sailboat, and when they couldn't find a font they liked, they came home, grabbed the Christmas card and had his own handwriting transferred to their skin.

Selon le vent

How to make Snurtle Sailboats in clay

1. Roll clay to 1/4 to 1/2 inch thickness
2. Use sailboat cookie cutter or template to cut sailboats in clay
3. Mold a hull that is proportional to sail
4. Affix sail to hull with slurry
5. Make a Snurtle sailor (see October)
6. Affix Snurtle to hull with slurry
7. Make piercings for any embellishments (i.e. anchor, mast, flags etc.)
8. Dry slowly and bisque fire
9. Under glaze and high fire
10. Set sail and enjoy your adventures around the world!

July – Summertime

*Beer Bratwurst and Beethoven
and other outdoor concerts*

Moosicians Limericks

A moose blew away on his tuba

And landed in worlds deep of scuba

A sprightly spring zephyr

Then hurricane weather

Washed him up on the warm shores of Cuba

There once was a moose who played strings

Used her bow to make smooth sounds - and PINGS

She played so divinely,

Her music sublimely

Was fit for all Jacks, Queens and Kings

How to make Music in Clay:

1. Roll out clay to approximately 1/4 inch thickness.
2. Freehand, trace, or copy the music element of your choice.
3. Cut out musical piece, using pin tool
4. Press stamps or draw lightly etched imagery into the musical element to create a unique design.
5. Smooth all edges. Use straw for placement of holes if used for hanging a wind chime, mobile, and tree ornament or wall art.
6. Let dry, covered in plastic on newsprint until bone dry.
7. Bisque, glaze, high-fire. Enjoy!

Find Music Note Cookie Cutters, or copy an image on paper, cut around it, and trace it into the clay.
Remember: Thicker lines are better than thinner lines for stability

How to make Moosicians ©:

1. Study a human anatomical model for proportions.
2. Mold body parts using your choice of clay (I usually use brown, black or red) for torso, head, arms, legs and antlers
3. Use slurry to attach parts. Prop to dry.
4. Add facial details as required
5. Add antlers or hair
6. Create instruments or props as required
7. Add clothing and accessories
8. Use tools for texture and detail
9. Cover and dry slowly
10. Bisque, glaze, high fire and enjoy the music!

August - Danielle

Passion, Education and Gentle Activism

CLAY IT FORWARD

I first met Danielle by telephone.

It was a weekend last fall, I believe; a leisurely Saturday. No shows to rush out to. Just an endless day of glazing, putzing, laundry and staring out the window, catching the tail ends of thought poems as they drifted through the ether.

When I answered the phone, a young woman asked about a workshop I was offering later in the day.
I panicked.

It's one of those fears...you know - leaving the baby in the car or at the grocery store checkout. Showing up at a gig without the clay. Not showing up for a gig...
We soon discovered she was looking at an old posting. I was relieved. We had a good laugh, I got her contact information and put her in touch with my friends and colleagues at the Sault Potters' Guild.

She sounded delightful. A student in her graduating year of the Natural Environment Technician – Conservation and Management program at Sault College, Danielle was curious to take a pottery class.
Our paths crossed again -this time in person - at the college during the Seedy Saturday event, where I was a vendor with my Clay It Forward program, and also during March Break for the Fishbowl Festival hosted by social entrepreneurs, Sam Decter and Nicole Dyble, proprietors of the Gore Street Cafe.

Danielle and her boyfriend, another graduating college student, brought a handful of friends and family visiting from southern Ontario to this community event celebrating all things Pisces.

From there, we got to talking more, and Danielle shared her vision of travelling to Indonesia next year to work at an Orangutan (people of the forest) Centre.

She talked about fund-raising during the summer, and I sent her home with a chunk of clay to start playing around with some ideas for pendants, charms or beads - things that could be made quickly and sell well.

I thought if she continued to take to the clay, she could join a guild or group when she returned home and continue with her production. On her phone, she also had an image of an orangutan sculpture she wanted to try...

Danielle returned to the NRC (neighbourhood resource centre) the following week for the Clay It Forward session, bringing with her a delightful assortment of charms, and I showed her how to put two pinch pots together as the base for her sculpture.

We kept in touch through social media, and Danielle kept me posted on her progress through images...her little guy was coming along quite nicely, and I told her to get a garlic press to make some orangutan hair...

Our next meeting was outside the Sault Potters' Guild where I returned her bisqued pendants and she glazed them. I suggested she document all her projects so she could leverage sales and increase fundraising opportunities by selling the images of her work in postcards, greeting cards, calendars, books etc.

While waiting for me, Danielle had visited some of the shops in the Co-op and was happy to find handmade soap free of palm oil.

She had brought literature about the ubiquitousness of Palm oil in so many of our consumer products and how the clear cutting of Palm trees in Indonesia and Malaysia is quickly wiping out habitat for the orangutans which call only two islands in the world home: Sumatra and Borneo.

Later that afternoon, I was invited to like Danielle's new Facebook page she had set up for her cause: Danielle Utan.
She took the plunge and made the next step on her mission real by sharing her vision and starting the ripple effect.

I love that I got to witness this unfolding of Danielle's dream and provide just one of the materials on which she will leave her mark.

How to make clay pendants to fund your life adventures.

1. Roll out a slab of clay to a thickness between 1/8 and 1/4 inch.
2. Using a pin tool, sharp skewer or small cookie cutter, cut the desired shape of your pendant.
3. Using stamps or other tools, design your pendant, keeping in mind where you will place the hole for the cord or chain.
4. Smooth all edges with a damp sponge or cloth.
5. Place hole for cord or chain at least 1/4 inch from edge to avoid cracking.
6. Cover with plastic and place on newsprint on flat surface to dry slowly.
7. Bisque fire when dry.
8. Glaze as desired. High fire.
9. Hang pendant on cord or chain.
10. Document. Sell. Repeat. Enjoy your travels!

How to make a clay orangutan to fund your life adventure

1. Find a good image or model of an orangutan to study.
2. Make some sketches from several angles to get the "feel" of your creature.
3. Make two equal pinch pots that fit snugly in the palm of your hand (we're keeping it small enough so it doesn't require an armature.
4. Using a toothbrush (or stiff paintbrush) and a little bit of clay slurry, attach the two pinch pots for the creature's body. Shape accordingly and insert a skewer to provide air release.
5. Add head with features. (You may want to hollow out part of the head if it seems too thick). Attach with brush and slurry when body has stiffened a bit.
6. Add arms, legs and detail
7. Add garlic pressed "hair" and/or scratch in hair-like pattern with skewer or sharp tool.
8. Cover with plastic and dry thoroughly.
9. Bisque, glaze and high fire.
10. Document. Sell. Repeat. Enjoy your travels!

September - Back to School

I always loved back to school.

I liked the routine of a school day, the new school supplies, the idea of a fresh start...

As a student, teacher, mother of students and mentor, I've always been drawn to the language arts.

I love dictionaries, grammar rules, etymology and spelling; I like to think that I have a knack of explaining the obscurities and mysteries of the dark corners of such to baffled students.

To that end, I've muddled about with some ideas to try to clarify some concepts through poems.

An anatomy of prepositions was first conceived when I was teaching ESL to a group of Mennonites of German descent who had moved from Mexico to Aylmer, a small town southeast of London, Ontario.

In my "Level 3 class", I had four generations from the same family. My group was strong in English, conversationally, and were working on strengthening reading and writing skills.

A common exercise was to have the students write new vocabulary words in sentences and paragraphs to improve familiarity, context and so on.

I've always remembered a classic sentence, written by a student named Margaret, that I vowed I'd use someday, somehow: The head grows between the ears.
Doesn't it just?
And so evolved "An anatomy of prepositions":

The head grows right between the ears

The nose betwixt the eyes

The chin above the collar bone

The knees below the thighs

The nails grow from the fingertips

The buds upon the tongue

The toes beyond the tibia

The spine ends at the bum

The lungs grow safe behind the ribs

The brain inside the skull

The pearly whites are rooted near

The crunching mandible.

Clay activity

I have been fortunate to receive many gifts from retiring teachers with whom I have done "Clay in the Classroom" workshops over the years. One gave me a bag full of thick, cardboard tubes that are perfect for mug making. Another gave me a great Styrofoam and fabric dragon that I hang in my studio as my kiln's fire spirit. Another gave me bags full of rubber stamps, including an anatomy set with bones, brains and organ. These stamps are great for units on archeology, Halloween and medicine and fit nicely with this poem.

Instructions:

1. Decide on a clay project: mug, plate, clock etc.
2. Roll out clay to desired shape about 1/4 inch thick
3. Use anatomy stamps and letter stamps to impress in the clay and to study the relationship of bones and various organs and their relation to each other using the "words that point": prepositions.
4. Bisque fire, glaze and high fire
5. Pay attention to how prepositions are used in writing. Recognize prepositional phrases to help de-mystify subject-verb agreement and other grammatical constructions as required by your schooling.

Alternate activity

1. Find a complete list of prepositions.
2. Make a sculpture of a person or animal or imaginary creature in clay.
3. Let dry, bisque fire, glaze and high fire
4. Practice using prepositions by noticing where parts of the body are in relation to others
5. Be aware of how prepositions are used to improve your own verbal and written communication skills.

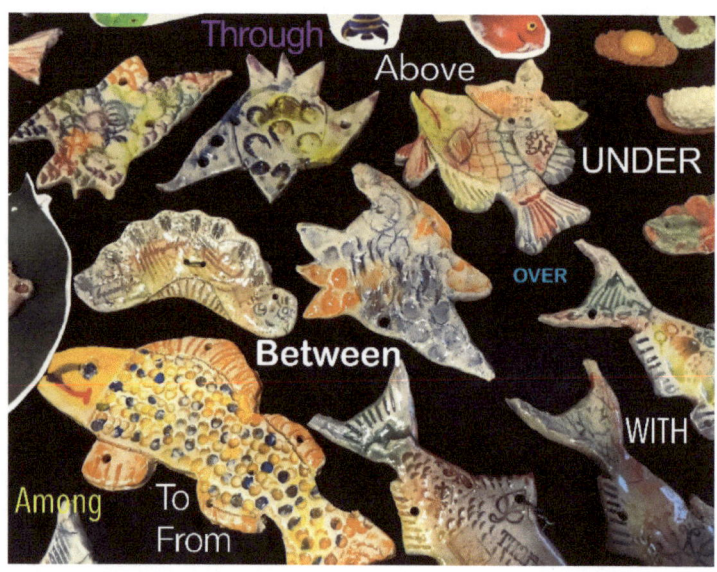

Party Hats for the Ball Family was conceived when my oldest daughter was just about four and I was compelled by her to make little paper party hats for her collection of rubber balls.

It was a delightful afternoon, and again, the title stuck with me for years and emerged recently in the following form:

The Ball Family

When her sister was a rolling heartbeat in my belly,
My daughter, aged three,
Asked if we could make party hats for the ball family.

35 balls came to the party at the dining room table.

Tennis balls,
Old-fashioned red, white and blue rubber balls
Souvenir balls with airplanes or dinosaurs or swirly bits of twirl
Suspended in some magical compound of clear bounce
Tiny jack balls
Baby bocce balls and bowling balls
Miniature baseballs, soccer balls, basketballs

Handsful of the sweetest little candy-coloured bouncers
From games and loot bags and plastic globes in mall dispensers

All corralled in a gossamer bag with a satin ribbon from Mama.

We made the party hats from any kind of paper:
Gift wrap, tin foil, coloured paper, paper coloured, scraps

We wrapped the paper into a cone,
And cut it where it would fit the ball
And taped it into place.

What a party!

Ever since that day,
When we three
Were such a huddle of closeness,
A bubble of party planning,
I've come to imagine,
Over the years,
The games the Ball Family
Might have played at their parties,
Their family reunions and assorted festive gatherings…

What if they invited a boxful of alphabet pasta
To play Ball Family Scrabble and Boggle
And Balderdash and Charades?

What if the letters made friends into words
And the Ball Family played hopscotch and leap frog
And Red Rover?

What if they all went to the beach in the summer
And wrote messages in the sand
Or on bark and leaves
 And slipped them into bottles
Or watched them wash out into the surf
Riding wild surfer waves
And the Ball Family had to skip
Like hard fast stones through the tides
 When the word lines got carried away
Like those dancing trains
At wedding parties?

Or what if, in the winter, the Ball Family put on their toques
And went outside as snow balls
And pelted sense
Into ice-cubed messages on frozen rivers and lakes
And amongst the stars?

And what if the Ball Family realized they could use their bouncy
Selves and pointing hats
To bring meaning –

Through their dots and dashes and marks and curves and glyphs
Of every imagining –

To the tumble, jumbled pile of letters, words and sentences
Like guests at wedding parties
That form those endless, dancing trains of thought;
The poems and shimmering prose,
Those heartfelt trains of soul and song,
Of jazz, of rhythm and blues
That track their ways onto pages
And screens and scores

To make a magic code

That I could write and you could read

And we'd both know the knowing.

And what if it all were true?

And who's to say it isn't so?

Now I've thought it
And written it.
And drawn it.
And told it.

Maybe it's as true as that huddle time so long ago

When we first made party hats for the Ball Family
And we shared a little bubble of knowing

There is always some tiny way to make a little sense of all the jumble...

Activity

1. Decide on a clay project: mug, plate, clock, etc.
2. Use rubber stamp punctuation marks (or create your own) to create designs and patterns in the clay
3. Use word and letter stamps - and the correct punctuation marks - to express a thought in clay.
4. Dry, bisque fire, glaze and high fire the project
5. Be aware of the correct use of punctuation marks in your writing

CLAY IT FORWARD

October - A Snurtle's Hallowe'en

One Snurtle shouts out "boo!" to you.

Two devilish Snurts play tricks.

Three scaredy cats high-tail it past

Four Jack-o-lanterns' wicks

Five haunted Snurtle houses glow

With six drip-flickering torches

And seven Snurts watch ghosts fly by

From eight creak-cracking porches.

Nine Snurtles holler "Trick or Treat!"

To neighbour, friend and fiend.

Ten twinkling stars blink from afar

This Snurtlish Hallowe'en

Thanks to my youngest sister, Michelle, Snurtles © were created in about 1992, a combination of snails and turtles, both of which were laborious and unsatisfactory in completion.

I was already smitten by the combination character, having created St. Mary's River Dinogans and Dragosaurs earlier, so these were fun little creatures once I figured it all out.

The figuring out led to a series of "How to make your own Snurtle"...or whatever creature...instructions, used as "Make and Take" kits in modelling clay in the Kids' Zone for Rotaryfest at Clergue Park in Sault Ste. Marie.

These kits were printed on brightly coloured papers for each creature, and they marked a marathon weekend the third weekend in July that started the summer my first daughter was born in 1994.

I was teaching summer school, and my husband would meet me at the bus with the screaming baby...she wouldn't take a bottle from him...we'd walk home, get her settled and get ready for the weekend.

My mom, a great crafter, organizer and baby lover helped me get my chaos in order, colour coding all the kits, packaging, sorting, making lists - all a far and irritating cry from my usual method of dumping things in bags and hoping for the best.

My dad and husband would be off somewhere telling jokes, drinking beer, eating peanuts, poring over crossword puzzles and trying to avoid "the project".

Thursday, Friday and Saturday were spent at the Kid Zone at Rotaryfest, chasing the shade of a 10 x 10 tent trying to keep sticky modelling clay cool enough to coerce into critter shapes.

Sunday we went to St Joseph Island for Art in the Park.

One year I did a float in the Rotary parade. Never again. Way too hot. And Queen Street's way too long to traipse along, tossing candies to the madding crowds.

It was memorable though: we had a four piece student band belting the tunes from the float, my mom and two daughters, by then had a kid's tent on the float stocked with candies, and a theatre friend had two dressed mimes promoting her summer theatre programs.

All for the love of a Snurtle!

Here's how to make one:

1. Make the Parts: Roll out a sausage coil for the body, roll out a thinner and longer sausage coil for the shell, create a small horn and a smaller tail to look like ice cream cones, create 4 feet, create a small pancake-shaped lip, create eyes and eyebrows.
2. Assemble the Parts: Form the body into an S-shape and put the tail onto the back, twist the coil into a spiral (like soft ice cream) and put on top of the body, put the feet under the body.
3. Add the features – the eyes, eyebrows, and lip
4. Finish by twisting the horn into a spiral and putting on the top of the head between the eyes. Finally, poke two nostrils into the face above the lip.
5. Voila! Your very own Snurtle ©!

CLAY IT FORWARD

November - Remembrance Day

When my husband was teaching, he'd invite his father, Bob Mihell Sr., to speak at the Remembrance Day service at the high school.

You could hear a pin drop, he said, so riveted were the kids to this man and his words, his command of the stage, his connection to the crowd.

My husband took over these duties himself, after his dad passed away just after Christmas in 1999, re-telling all the stories he'd heard over the years, starting with the impossible anguish his grandparents would have endured watching all four of their sons going off to serve - and the miracle in welcoming all four of them home.

Natural raconteurs, both these men could hold court in classrooms, bar rooms and board rooms, so charismatic, charming, irreverent, quick and funny that to be within earshot, was to be captivated.

One of the stories my husband added to the roster unfolded when he was about 12.

He remembered travelling with his uncle and family one summer, and stopping in to see an old war chum. The two men's lives had taken very different paths. Uncle, like his brothers, had a comfortable middle class life; his friend, a native man, did not.

Yet Bob, then a boy, remembers being struck by the camaraderie of the two in each other's unmasked company - the honesty, the equality, the brotherhood, the trust and bond still strong, years later and worlds apart as they talked their way back to their shared past, as young, frightened men in an unfathomable adventure.

Remembering.

We are, by turns, reciprocating partners in this timeless dance between story-teller and story catcher: speaker and listener, writer and reader, performer and audience.

We are compelled to document stories - great and small, magnificent and trivial, our own and others'.

Telling and retelling. Giving form and longevity to the ephemeral. Leaving our marks. Knowing we mattered and somebody cared.

My business partner in Great Lakes Basin and Splash Tile, Katie Alton, of Engine9Design, felt moved to document her Great Aunt Joan's story, and pitched it, successfully to CBC's Living Out Loud with Chris Howden. You can find it there, posted on July 17, 2015.

In her 90's, "Auntie J" is a rock solid, honky-tonk playing, hymn singing bundle of Christian energy, wearing a trademark blonde bun, putting her life in her

Lord's hands, and loving Katie fiercely and loyally, even though she's not a believer.

Over lunch recently, I asked Katie what it was about her aunt that compelled her to record the piece:

"She's just so amazing and exotic. She and Uncle Arnold lived in California for 25 years - most of my life. I remember going on a trip and visiting them when I was in grade 1. It was beautiful there, and she had these incredible things growing in her garden - all kinds of fruit trees, lemon trees, avocados...but she was thrilled to be able to move back to Algoma, to walk again through the northern bush, and kick the crisp leaves.

She's my grandmother's older sister, so she reminds me of her. They have the same voice, but Aunt Joan's is a higher register. She has great stories. She was a school teacher in Echo Bay before she was married, and she roomed and boarded in a house with a couple. It was terrible and cold - she drank cod liver oil out of the bottle. She was - and is - always conscious of her health, since she had Scarlet Fever and almost died as a girl. She used to own goats when they lived on their little farmhouse on the land off Lake Street.

Her house is beautiful and tasteful. She has a collection of angels. She dresses very well and still dyes her hair blond, and wears it in a trademark bun with pins and embellishments. She's always on the go, running up and down the stairs, coming and going. People are in and out of her house, visiting and praying.

She's very musical, singing and playing the piano and organ at the church and women's coffee hour. She still gives lessons and everyone knows her as Grammy Joey.

Very business-minded, she used to run a furniture store.

She and Uncle Arnold never had any children which was a shame, I think, because she's so good with children and young people. He was an accountant and passed away eight years ago. They were good friends; he was opinionated and political, but everyone put up with him because he was a jokester, too.

I remember he had special stationery that said, 'From the desk of Arnold'. He'd send you a letter with a joke on it that asked something like, 'What do you call a cow after she's had a calf?'

Then, you'd have to wait for the next letter with the answer: 'decaffeinated.'"

Two clay projects I like to use to remember people by documenting and retelling their stories are Masks and Mug Shots.

How to make a clay mask.

1. Roll out a clay slab about 1/4-1/2 inch thick
2. After studying masks and making some preliminary sketches, cut your mask in the desired size and shape.
3. Give your mask shape by draping it over a form (wadded newspaper, plaster molds, bowls or platters covered in cloth to prevent sticking)
4. Alternately, press the clay into a lined mask mold.
5. Use tools to score designs and texture into the mask as desired
6. Use small chunks of clay to add features to your mask as desired. Remember to roughen the two surfaces and add a bit of slurry when joining one piece of clay to another, such as the nose.
7. Use a pin tool or skewer for any piercings, such as holes for affixing wire for hanging or adding embellishments such as hair or beads
8. Trim and smooth rough edges.
9. When leather hard, allow mask to finish drying over wads of paper (remember that clay shrinks as it dries and will crack if left on the mold)
10. Bisque, Glaze, High fire and tell the story of the person that inspired this mask.

CLAY IT FORWARD 109

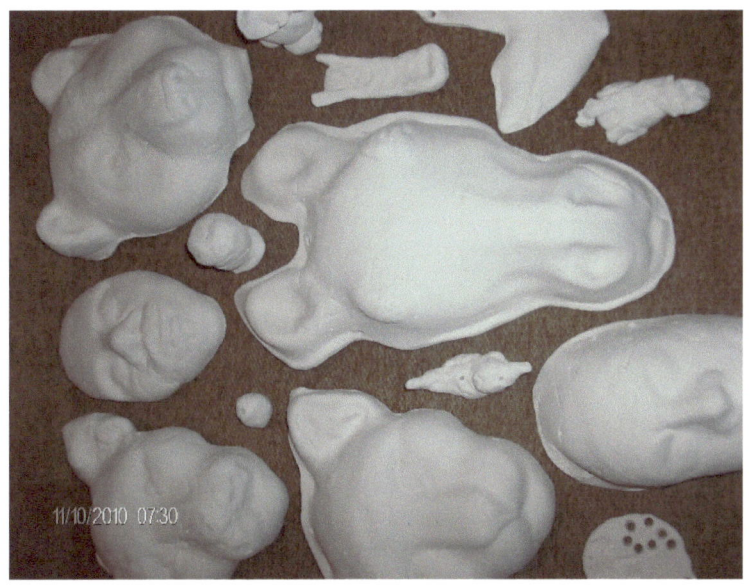

December – Elventide

Elventide - Community Christmas

The upshot....

On the fifth day of Elventide, a Snurtle gave to me

Five porcupines

Four white-tailed deer

Three bears in dens

Two chickadees

and a Moose rack of antlers, pointy.

On the sixth day of Elventide, a Snurtle gave to me

Six screeching Jays

■■

Seven sleepy squirrels
Eight plump wild turkeys
Nine caribou
Ten timber wolves
Eleven leopard frogs.
Twelve great-horned owls.

Cut out buttons or shapes as in other months, bisque, and under glaze with holiday colours, follow instructions and have a wonderful holiday season with loved ones.

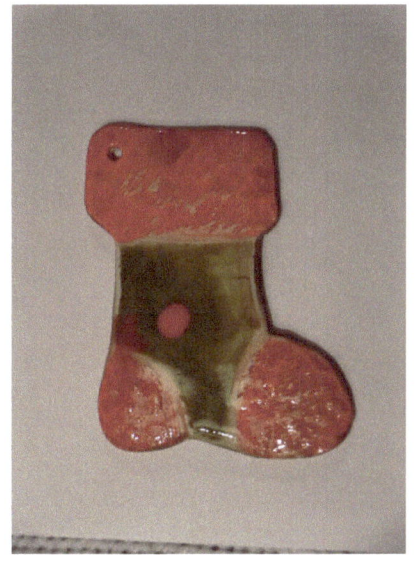

ABOUT THE AUTHOR

Cass Cameron (aka Sandra Hodge) lives, writes, teaches and practices Clay it Forward in Sault Ste. Marie, Ontario, Canada.

Thanks to Porter, she can be with family and friends in her birthplace of Toronto in just over an hour, and in the same time again, be in her hometown of Orillia for more visiting.

Follow the mud and magic at
www.clayitforward.ca
and like us on Facebook/clayitforward.

www.ingramcontent.com/pod-product-compliance
Lightning Source LLC
Chambersburg PA
CBHW042304150426
43197CB00001B/9